WHY I SING THE BLUES

Why I Sing the Blues

L y r i c s & P o e m s

edited by Jan Zwicky and Brad Cran

Why I Sing the Blues
Copyright © 2001 by Smoking Lung Press

First Edition

Published in 2001 by
Smoking Lung Press
#103-1014 Homer Street
Vancouver BC
V6B 2W9

Distributed through
Arsenal Pulp Press
#103-1014 Homer Street
Vancouver BC
V6B 2W9
www.arsenalpulp.com

Cover design and typesetting by Brad Cran

The Audio portion of this project was made possible by the generous support of The Mac-Mc-Zwick Society for Just About Anything That'll Sound Good on the CD. The publisher expresses thanks.

Printed and Bound in Canada

NATIONAL LIBRARY OF CANADA CATALOGUING IN PUBLICATION DATA

Zwicky, Jan, 1955-
Why I Sing the Blues

Poems.
ISBN 1-894442-01-6

I. Cran, Brad, 1972- II. Title.
PS8599.W53W49 2001   C811´.54   C2001-911409-5
PR9199.3Z95W49 2001

CONTENTS

FOREWORD

This project got its start on a particularly sunny afternoon when, neither lovesick, unemployed, or hungover, I was tidying up the living room. I'd been listening to Robert Johnson a few days earlier, and the booklet with the biography and recording dates and timings for the tracks was lying on one of the speakers. I picked it up to put it back in its box, flipping it open absent-mindedly to the transcriptions of the lyrics. I read; and kept on reading. It wasn't that they were unfamiliar to me – we'd had the recording for years. But it was the first time I'd registered how powerful those lyrics were as poetry – what an astonishing *poetic* form the blues was. I wondered if it might be possible for poets to write in that form, even if they'd never tuned a guitar or tightened a drumskin in their lives.

A few years and several fifths of Jack Daniels later, you hold in your hands the answer to that question. The process of solicitation was rag-tag and word-of-mouth, and the pieces that started filtering in ranged from traditional 8- and 12-bar blues to experiments that pushed the limits of the genre. Some folks found that writing lyrics didn't suit them and wound up writing *about* the blues instead. But everyone was excited. Maybe it was the basic melancholy of poets, maybe it was the long winters, maybe it was the pun splicing the off-side rule with verse metrics: in any event, it turned out to be a project that had been waiting to happen. We had many more submissions than we were able to include in the present volume; and we hope that it represents not only a quintessence but the beginning of a trend.

Odd though it may sound, blues poetry turns out to have more in common with haiku than *Howl*. It's a strict, minimalist form, with a classical vocabulary of images and set phrases. (The word "alone", for example, should always be rhymed with "telephone". And no matter who answers, the news is never good.) The joy of such a form is the subtle effects that can be achieved precisely because we think we know what's coming next. Irony, of course, is the emotional driveshaft of choice, that edgy blend of wit and despair.

i

One poet did think the idea was crazy: didn't I know the blues was an *oral* art form? How did I imagine poets were going to write lyrics uncoupled from their musical incarnations? They'd be the literary equivalent of the tin in bronze, or the baking soda in an unbaked cake. What would be the point?

The point, I think, is that the mind's ear is larger than the literal eye – and that that's what those Johnson lyrics showed me: they were poems that stood on their own, black on the white page, even though Johnson himself never wrote them down. They could be this because good writing, of any sort, is never more than a finger pointing at the moon, an attempt to move beyond the page, and words, into experience. There is no reading without imagination. The lyrics collected here invite you to listen to them as poems in their own right, and also to listen through them, to the guitars, the harps and keyboards, the horns and gutbuckets, in whose imagined existence they step up and sing. You're the composer here. Hum or thump or twang along. Maybe don't quit your day job just yet, but feel free to phone in sick.

Black on the white page: there's the other question this project raises. The blues is an art form whose origins are intimately linked with the experience of racial oppression. It's one thing for middle-class folks of European ancestry to listen to the blues, quite another to get lost in them. What could white, free, twenty-first-century Canadians have to say that wouldn't amount to a Disneyfication of the form and its history?

It is my hope that this volume shows that they can say what the blues has taught them, and in so doing, render homage. The blues is among the most political of art forms. Elsewhere, art and politics tend to get together for a one-night stand; in the blues, they're married. The blues is not simply the expression of the experience of oppression, it is an attempt to heal that experience: a naming so hot and salty it draws the poison, so true it lances its heart.

It is the greatness of the blues that it speaks not only to particular oppressions but to oppression itself: the experience of being powerless in the face of systemic injustice. It is undoubtedly true that white North Americans have, as a class, felt the bite of such injustice less keenly than most; it is also true that they are the beneficiaries of its perpetuation in many quarters. As individuals, however, it is possible to recognize and to resist inherited thoughtlessness. A number of the poems in this volume are protests against global corporate capitalism, against the suburbanification it depends on, and the environmental devastation it breeds; others, like many early African-American blues, are protests against the cosmic injustice, the can't-live-with-'em-can't-live-without-'em, of sex; still others protest the betrayals of the body and the abandonments of old age. The intention in every case has been to celebrate the cathartic capacities of the art form, and to honour the spirit of those who gave birth to it.

My thanks to everyone who helped: Charles Wright for his generous response to a letter out of nowhere, Colin Macleod for timely inspirations and financial support, Bill Johnson for his enthusiasm, Don McKay for his superb advice, and most especially to Brad Cran, who wanted it to happen, and so it did.

Jan Zwicky
Victoria, June 5, 2001

Why I Sing the Blues

SPEED BLUES JUNKET INTO HARMONICA

Ken Babstock

A face cast up where metal birds ignite.
O hang this neck with penance, with retreat,
             that we not start fights.

[*Harmonica. Harmonica as argument over last morsel. As sway-back
mare. As medical chart. Weather
fronts exhaust themselves peeling away over
Harmonica. Harmonica
grifts, braggadocio, then with its graven plastic head kicked
in. Stove stoked by Harmonica
breeds left-behindness sends a postcard.*]

* * *

He ate up all her chicken, wine and rice
without her knowing, pinched it from its place.
             He wasn't to her nice.

[*Harmonica as stand-in for long shot at Gethsemane. As long
since uncut forelocks. Threshing
machines mowing in tandem four abreast shave
Harmonica before going
out. Harmonica gives Hiss kiss on temple settling into its own
UnderIce. As picked bluebell, pines
away. Harmonica pouring out tall stacks yellowish.*]

* * *

Whatever strife there was to begin with's now double.
He thinks his manservant, practical, worthy, able,
             but, Lord, unbearable.

[*Harmonica grey-beard, Calabri-Yau hoards Harmonica's seven
dimensions. Tendering resignation
Harmonica sugars the gas tank. As hold-up. As
language-death stalking the brain
base kitten-blind. Nobody touch Harmonica. As a long wait for noone.*]

1

As watercress. As not what you ordered.
Harmonica's thoroughness a tracheotomy in tool shed.]

* * *

Lament lament lament lament lament.
It goes this way until 'ere long it's *went* –
                    and where his interment?

[*As timepiece, melting sundial. As thought emergent, Cannibal*
Harmonica flings hooks last ditch
Harmonica into the elusive meat of a moment trying
to shore up the flood of what's
going. As the stringed seam of a bean. Harmonica stray dogs about
town. Foot-prints Harmonica in fresh
snow, there they go. Harmonica admits to there being
not one answer. As too many.]

thats a lot uv
suitcases 4 onlee a whil

bill bissett

ium
sittin heer
all alone uv kours
n cud I wundr
wher yu went?
wher yu ar?
wher yu got 2? nobodee knoes time moovs
as slow as sand up a hill

ium
sittin heer n
th barge moovs slowr
thn hope down
th watr way in
2 th harbor

ium layin heer
n th dreems cascade
sew funnee with
yu on th othr side
on th othr side

in th dreem
in ths town
thees tracks on
my mind
funnee how yu
sd it o didint
i tell yu ium
leevin 4
a whil   eezee street nevr cums not
heer not on ths erth

o didint i
tell yu ium
leevin 4 a whil
no i sd i

3

            dont recall yu
    sayin that what a
            ball ths is i herd   time moovs
            yu say   as slow as
        i dont know   sand up
      how things change   a hill
    that's a lot uv
            suitcases
        4 onlee a
                whil

            is it i
    lookd at sum   o didint I tell yu
    wun 2 long   o didint I tell yu
    undr th willow   o didint I tell yu
      thats a lot uv
      suitcases 4
        onlee a whil

      embrace th moon
    hug th dreem embrace   eezee street
        th long street   nevr cums not
      with no wun on it   on ths erth
                huh   not heer

            thats a lot
      uv suitcases
    4 onlee a
            whil

    o didint I tell yu

                                    4

AFTER BEING ASKED   *Shane Book*
TO WRITE A BLUES LYRIC –

A simple stillness comes, unpleated secretly
its shiny clasps removed.
Something settling – flicker of a song
ending,
              some deepest
some darkest heart
almost covering:
                        a coat
                              a shawl
                                      draped easily –
a knowledge, like a knowledge
                              that some feeling
should probably come *after.*

Has it always been night?

I am at the river.
                  The slicking sound
in the dark rippling – what would you call it – a throat? You
my first ear, what would you call it?

I came to the river
to listen.
          The broken
line of land
the stopless water (the book said)
was where the song comes together
the variable rumor of air begins –
and how does it do this

*

He walked into the river

Rock me baby

"They sold me down the river"

5

A unit of

As in is it deep?

They call it stormy Monday

(separation and connect…)

A unit of Mississippi mud

As in sold down the river to a plantation in Mississippi

Rock me baby

A unit of

*

I will sit down.
I will try to hear.
I will try to hear the patient cycle
of the whirlpools – water spooling
loose a few seconds
the little O's cruising open
in a soft popping rush
                      a curled leaning
across
        (this is all made up for you, my inner ear, remember, it is dark)
the sooty surface
                desiring, desiring…

*

If there was a figure in the river

If I don't find my baby, ain't gonna let my airplane down

A piece of

A gathering

6

How deep is it?

Discharging itself into the sea

The confluence of river and sea is

Do you think it is cold?

I pass a million people I can't tell who I meet

The high water mark

*

A shape moving.
On the opposite bank and
from the left.
Darker than the basic
                darkness, as if blacklit
by a faint light (where, where)
or, a glowing away from
by some crushing out
of light –
A shape moving.
A taut line
            connecting it
to a second
lower
more animal lope,
the unit
            drifting to the right
a procession fading
into the surrounding unillumination
until there is
            only the spiked
space
made in the air
for a tree – strange and fruitless in this late Iowa autumn –
and a dim line, the rectangular top of a
(you love the strict geometry)
                building –

7

*

"Sent up the river"

The river does not run through anything

The river runs around stone

Say the train is at the station and my mind is made up to go

The stone in one

(of the sparrow)

The one in stone

Sent up the Hudson River from New York to Sing Sing

To break into the stone in *one*

I feel like Rockin' till the rooster crows for days

*

It is so dark
I can't see my dark hands.
There is a feeling now
on the river.
There is a barely perceptible wind
down over it
a certain smell,
something growing old.
It is dark.
You,
      with your tiny instruments
fluttering
ungodly
mastering a movement
catching the whispers
with your net
            like a diction,

8

you must
believe me.
You
with your
busy work – the stitching
                    of air on air with your thread of listening –
how is that made to measure?

I wanted to know
where the song was from.
What if the book said
to look
in the mud?
You must
believe me. There was once
a story here. I have
no way to prove this.
Is there a spotted nest?
Is there a mud fortress carved by slow water?

*

The ancestors

To break into

They worshipped the one in stone

To break into

Well it's getting dark, everything seem to fade out

They worship the

(The water laps the bank in a gentle rhythm)

To break into

A relatively short

A trifle

An insignificant sum

The ancestors

Everything seem to be fading out

*

The river bank is mud.
The mud suctions the flat surface of my shoe.
In the mud there are *no showy spurred flowers of various colors*
The mud of a flooded field and the mud of a single ditch –
and after water and after sun –
and after the battle is over.
The mixing in of blood and cartilage.
The mud holds the foot a little.
The mud slides the foot a little.

A whirlpool opens and
                    what comes out?

*

The river bank is changing slowly by a process we can't see

How can you be so evil

This is an oxbow lake, this used to be a bend in the river

Rock me as easy as you can

Flowing through a certain portion of the earth's surface

Singing for very little money

White bubbles of river scum, careening along the dark surface

Some time I don't know what, some time I don't know what in this world to do

*

Far off hinge-shot howlings of a train
air forced into the night
pushed to take its place
and the rip in the seam of the sky sings –
Is that how it happens?
Is there always pain? I've forgotten.
Does the rumble come first? I've forgotten.

The train sounds
                    like it is coming closer
festering, improvising, entering
                                    the air
In the old stories [old songs] isn't there always a train coming?
[In the old stories [old songs] isn't the train always coming?]
[In the [song] story there is always a train coming...]

*

I'm down
looking at the mud now
(where the book told me)
the sticky darkness
                    sucks and squenches my shoe
when I lift it.
Rotted grass smell
burrowing down in the ground smell
to lie there
                and dream in the coolness
of air lifting off
water,
the tendrils of grass (I have to imagine this)
as fluttering notes
(counterpoint to train rumble)

I put my hand where I think the water is.
I'm waiting for the sound
you told me
would be there

in the hunch
of air
rippling over
the bunched dead leaves
caught in the current
by an overhanging tree – something
caught
in the doubling back
of current around an object
that protrudes
such as stump
such as rock
such as my hand

in the water now (the surprising warmth).
I think I feel the way the water spills
back and around
curling out from both edges
at angles to the other water...

There is something white
on the water now, foam, blurred
in the low light
curling in
on itself
curling in
the back eddy of a stone-shape
near the bank –
tucked in a long streaming line
behind the stone
it curls its white body
the formal white going on and on
and eventually the curling
the shape and the consciousness dissipates –
the water –
        a faceless deep
breathing chest
        feels warm
and the smell
            (part acid part urge)
and the small wind...

*

I'm going to show you that I'm no monkey man

Is it shallow if

Does contact differ from touch

Who has the water been

Have you ever, ever wanted someone and you thought they didn't want you

This, this here is, erosion

A trifle

An insignificant sum.

*

There are even little almost-waves lapping against my hand!
Are you still with me, my inner ear?
It is just mud and water here.
A weighted darkness over everything.
The quavering of your tiny motors.
I watch and watch.
The sound is nowhere.
The train is gone. If I count to ten, will I remain
in the mud? If I can't to ten…
I pull my hand out.
The air surrounds
                    turns, clicks
            creatured movement
little knife tips dotting the flesh
        granules of
molecules of
some indivisible thing of –
deeper and deeper
reclamation
of whatever is in there –

13

trying to suck it all out
from where
it no longer belongs...

Out of the water my hand goes cold —

COLD RIVER

Adam Chiles

for Angelina Romero

Across the Rio Grande I went
across the freezing waters,
paid a man a thousand bucks
to swim the Texas border

but I got Massaya in my heart

crossed it with my children
crossed it with the Lord
paid a man a beggars wage
to reach the promised land

but I got Massaya in my heart

cold river, cold river
we crossed you on a rubber tire
sweet river we crossed you
Texas jail on the other side

but I got Massaya in my heart

and tonight a man is drunk
in the City of Flowers
tonight, children, your father
will not dream of you

tonight in the City of Flowers

cold river, cold river
we crossed you on a rubber tire
sweet river we crossed you
Texas jail on the other side.

KING BEE BLUES

George Elliott Clarke

I'm an ol' king bee, honey,
Buzzin' from flower to flower.
I'm an ol' king bee, sweets,
Hummin' from flower to flower.
Women got good pollen,
I gets some every hour.

There's Lily in the valley
And sweet honeysuckle Rose too;
There's Lily in the valley
And sweet honeysuckle Rose too.
And there's pretty, black-eyed Susan,
Perfect as the night is blue.

You don't have to trust
A single Black word I say.
You don't have to trust
A single Black word I say.
But don't be surprised
If I sting your flower today.

TO SELAH

George Elliott Clarke

The butter moon is white
Sorta like your eyes;
The butter moon is bright, sugah,
Kinda like your eyes.
And it melts like I melt for you
While it coasts 'cross the sky.

The black highway uncoils
Like your body do sometimes.
The long highway unwinds, mama,
Like your lovin' do sometimes.
I'm gonna swerve your curves
And ride your centre line.

Stars are drippin' like tears,
The highway moves like a hymn;
Stars are drippin' like tears, beau'ful,
The highway sways like a hymn.
And I reach for your love,
Like a burglar for a gem.

RAINY LADY

Lynn Coady

Sold that rainy lady
possibilities
Sold that rainy lady
gentle summer's breeze
Sold that rainy lady
all that she'd allow

But you can't sell that lady
nothing now.

Sold that rainy lady
weed-fields all in bloom
Told that rainy lady
They'll be diamonds, soon
Told that rainy lady
not to ask me how.

And you can't sell that lady
nothing now.

Sold that rainy lady
sun+moon+stars
Sold that rainy lady
Spinster-ladies' cars
Told that rainy lady
smile was a scowl

But you can't sell that lady
nothing now.

Good-bye rainy lady
get myself some other
lady
You can't sell that lady
nothing now.

I can't sell that lady nothing now.

THE CALM CASTRATION
CALLING IT QUITS FOREVER
I'M THROUGH BLUES

Brad Cran

Knew this kid back in school.
Teased this kid, we were cruel.
Knew this kid back in school.
Hid everytime we went to the pool.

One Nut Nelson who fell on a fence.
One Nut Nelson was swimming pool tense.
One Nut Nelson crushed pre-prime.
But One Nut Nelson's troubles weren't half as bad as mine.

Oh One Nut, see me now.
Oh One Nut, show me how.
Oh One Nut, love makes little sense.
Oh One Nut, boost me up that fence.
Oh One Nut, do it nice.
Oh One Nut, do it twice.

Heart sick?
No, no dick.
Eunuch.
Yeah.

Heart sick?
No, no dick.
Eunuch.
Yeah.

One Nut. No Nut. Baby I'm gone.
One Nut. No Nut. Now I'm alone.
One Nut. No Nut. I'm coming home.

One Nut Nelson who fell on a fence.
One Nut Nelson was swimming pool tense.
One Nut Nelson crushed pre-prime.
But One Nut Nelson's troubles weren't half as bad as mine.

TWO TIMIN' TREE   *Brad Cran*
TRASH BLUES

Dowery not coming
Love junket sunk
My baby's in the mountains
My feet are out of luck

I got the Blues
But I ain't ever been to Chicago
I got the Blues
But I ain't ever been to New Orleans
My baby left me for a treeplanter
My baby sleeps beneath the trees

Oh Lord I see her in the forest
Oh Lord she skinny dips the lake
Oh Lord bring her home
Let her shovel break

I got the Blues
But I ain't ever been to Chicago
I got the Blues
But I ain't ever been to New Orleans
My baby's on a bus to Smithers
But I have bigger dreams

One day I'll ride up
One day I'll ride out
One day she's going to know
What I'm all about

I got the Blues
But I ain't ever been to Chicago
I got the Blues
But I ain't ever been to New Orleans
My baby digs holes all day
Doesn't think of me inbetween

Yeah her new lover's got a tongue ring
But I swear I pleased my baby fine
Yeah her new lover's got big feet
Two sizes bigger than mine

Oh Lord let me have her
Oh Lord strike him down
Oh Lord take my pain
Send me out of this town

I got the Blues
But I ain't ever been to Chicago
I got the Blues
But I ain't ever been to New Orleans
Just Missisippi-Squamish
And those Memphis-Ladner dreams

Oh Lord I swear I'll travel
Oh Lord I'll not travel in vain
Oh Lord she'll hear I'm travelling
And she'll want to be mine again

I got the Blues
But I ain't ever been to Chicago
I got the Blues
But I ain't ever been to New Orleans
I hear blues in the mountains
I hear blues in the streams

Oh Lord tell me straight
If you were up in those trees
Would you keep planting
Or would you dream of New Orleans

There's rednecks in the hollow
There's hippies in the bar
When she asks where I am
Lord send me long and far

I got the Blues
But I ain't ever been to Chicago
I got the Blues
But I ain't ever been to New Orleans
My baby's in the mountains
My baby sleeps beneath the trees

WAITING FOR THE   *Lorna Crozier*
PHONE TO RING

No word for days. To be exact, three,
and I have you seedy, hotel-dead
on a carpet soaked with piss and whiskey.
Here, the maple's shouting red

and I have you seedy, hotel-dead.
Fall's the time to fall down hard.
Here, the maple's shouting red
in our otherwise quiet yard.

Fall's the time to fall down hard.
A hawk drops heavy from the sky.
In our otherwise quiet yard
I begin to count six ways to die.

A hawk drops heavy from the sky;
flies mend holes inside a plum.
I begin to count six ways to die
though six ways for you add up to one.

Flies mend holes inside a plum.
The maple's leaves are birthing cries.
Six ways to do it add up to one
and night falls fast from a neon eye.

The maple's leaves are a birthing cry.
Whiskey and piss soak into the floor.
Light falls fast from a neon eye.
No word for days. To be exact, four.

"GOD ALWAYS RAINS ON MY PICNIC": A HURTIN' COUNTRY BLUES

Lorna-Jean Crozier

Chorus:

God always rains on my picnic.
He always drops a fly in my wine.
He leaves me in the lurch even when I go to church.
So why should I love him all the time.

Most days I sit at home awful lonely;
most nights I sit at home awful sad.
So if you're really there above the stars in your easy chair,
why do you leave me feeling so damn bad.

The Reverend he dropped by and he lingered.
He said, "Woman take your life in your hands."
But it keeps slipping through my shaky fingers.
Like a busted egg timer's grains of sand.

(Chorus.)

He left me as you know for another.
He left me as you know for his wife.
Or was it true he left me for my brother?
It gets so confusing in this life.

Well, I packed up a box of self pity
and I shoved it right under my bed.
Lord, why did you make me so pretty
and not put a thought in my head.

(Chorus.)

FROSTY PORCH BLUES

Lynn Davies

Cat on the porch, I know you hear the wind
       in the leaves on the ground.
Another cold-paw season coming
       and nowhere to walk

except the paths I'll shovel to the woodpile,
       the road and for you.
Hey cat, if a train ever comes through
       this damn town,

we'll hop it, the rails warming up, rolling
       us south together.
Winter's a big room for worries, cat.
       How to pay the bills,

dry boots out in time, will the roads disappear
       again tomorrow.
Ice in your water bowl and my knees, days
       and days inside.

Hey cat, would you consider wings?
       Rare birds, you and I,
above the trees already bare and days
       going up in smoke.

We could follow the wild geese south,
       mess up their V.
No worries cat, nothing to fall into
       but the sky.

BLUES FOR A
THOUSAND CUSHIONS

Barry Dempster

World update: encephalitis
claims another brain in Peru
while the streets of Des Moines, Iowa

flow like Parisian sewers.
Just another Sunday afternoon,
the earth throwing a hurly-burly

in Guam, the Body bleeding into
Africa, the poet and his wife
out shopping for a sofa.

A newsman says, *two million*
a salesman, $799.
Rows and rows of leather, chintz,

cotton twill. Southwestern,
vanilla, William Morris vines.
A thousand cushions

to pamper our bones.
Do you have this in gold?
a Filipino family asks.

Love seats beckon,
cushions soft as flesh.
Sectionals to rearrange us

until we're out of breath.
An easy chair numbing
the whole of my spine.

Will it float? I almost ask,
bulletproof, built-in brave?
Will it hold me as I die,

I mean really hold me?
Wanting so much to buy
a little peace, beyond it all.

Update, north Toronto: man
disappears in blue-striped couch,
no bother, no casualties.

FALLING AND FALLING BLUES

Adam Dickinson

Nothing falls down easily;
snow gets ripped in the pines.
I'm not very good at catching
your eye.

Deer bed down under apple trees;
I can see them open-mouthed.
I can't speak to you
this loud.

If I were a kind of tall grass
I'd string into your room;
I'd practice being a piano,
a loom.

In my descending stems,
I can only play caprice;
lie among the apple cores
with me.

BUSH BLUES

John Donlan

(tuning: Vestapol)

My old neighbour made his own canoe
Man had the how, he carved his own canoe
Peeled off birch bark and sewed it like a shoe.

Try paddling now you're swamping in the wake
Big power boats, they swamp you in their wake
All that oil sure don't calm the lake.

Where's all the frogs that used to sing so sweet?
Every summer, sang this boy to sleep?
You can't find one green frog in all B.C.

Where's all the salmon, killer whales would eat?
Whales killing sea otters, orcas got to eat.
Whale can't open tins like you and me.

Last wolves in Banff Park, dying fast and slow
In four-lane traffic, dying fast and slow
You can't teach a wolf to cross the road.

Too many people, everyone says so
Too many people, everyone says so
Wish I never lived to see the wild things go.

one   *Stan Dragland*
      two
            one two three

TWELVE BARS

THE DUKE OF DUCKWORTH

Got the blues, but I'm too damn mean to cry

Being here right now with my feet in these socks, in these very shoes
resting on that blue patch of rug, the rug laid down on that new birch
floor – it's very strange. Wearing *these* clothes today rather than any of the
others hanging in my closet or lying in my drawers. Sitting on this couch
and glancing into exactly that and no other blue sky where it meets the
deeper blue ocean just at that grey band of cloud I won't ever see again. A
jet trailing jet stream far above. Strange that for this one instant in all the
millions of unregarded moments passing I should *know* I'm here, now,
with the sun bright on the green, the maroon, the grey, the rust and the
blue, all the clapboard houses stepped down Victoria towards Gower. That
I should *be* seeing it all and hearing the hammers on that renovating house
on the corner down there over the grand hum of the city. Lucky to be
here now, period.

        Woke up from a week of the blues, when I couldn't get away from
myself at all. Only so far as keeping an eye on the dog after she shat all
over three floors of the house. One bad week alone with my miserable
lonesome and that goddamn dog with her guilty eyes.

30

THE YELLOW DORY

Nobody knows you when you're down and out

"Welcome to St. Johns," says Fergus O'Byrne from the stage. Simon told him at the break we're here from Ontario and now he's addressing our table. "Thanks for coming out. We appreciate it. Just don't take any of our jobs." This gets a laugh. Fergus O'Byrne and Dermot O'Reilly, two thirds of the legendary folk group, Ryan's Fancy. At the end of the evening we approach the stage with thanks, and I don't know any better than to make a joke. "We promise not to take any of your jobs," I say, "but we *have* picked a few of your blueberries." I thought that would be a tiny bit funny – it wasn't the moon of humour I was shooting at – but Fergus O'Byrne hasn't a clue what I'm talking about. He just stares at me through those round, wire-rimmed glasses that looked funky all night but now seems vaguely teutonic. I'd like to blame the silence on him since I'm only returning a remark he made himself not thirty minutes ago. But I blame my miserable self. Middle-aged and aint got no sense yet hardly. If I had a dollar for every strained silence I've created in my lifetime, I'd be rich. Have mercy, I'd be a rich man today.

THE PETER EASTON

When I get you in my sights
Boom, Boom, out goes the light

Ron Hynes wrote "No Change" with Murray MacLauchlan to say how hard it is living in a too-small town with no prospects. In the song, St. John's is emptied right out. Everybody gone somewhere else, looking for work.

> You could fire off a cannon
> At the top of Long's Hill
> And a Gulliver's Taxi
> May be all that you'd kill

But the streets were not completely empty that time I was out for a run in December '97, finally on the flat after the climb up Long's Hill, just past Ches's Fish and Chips when a hard-packed snowball smacked into the side of my head. And whoever it was had led me so perfectly was gone. Vanished. No witnesses. You could fire off a cannon. Shit! But I shook it off – what the hell, it's only winter sports – and started up Pennywell. And pretty soon I started to feel better than I had before I got hit. That was an excellent throw, after all: small moving target, follow-through cut short on account of having to duck out of sight. There must be some kind of lesson here. There must be something we can learn. Yes there is, and here it comes: when you take a mean shot to the head and yet admire the asshole who did it, you've got to be *some* kind of a loser.

THE FAT CAT

You got to come on in my kitchen

To hear the legendary Roger Howse. Stuart says no one plays the blues any better. We think Stuart knows. He and Janet first heard Roger Howse at the Bull and Bear just after they got married, when they were poor as church mice. They didn't mean to go in there at all, with only a buck seventy-five to their name, but somebody hauled them in and somehow they drank until closing time on just that buck seventy-five. There was a moose head hanging on the wall, Janet says, with a red light in one eye and a green light in the other. This was about twenty years ago. We're hearing about it in the kitchen of 70 Prescott, once owned by Johnny Burke, "the bard of Prescott Street." Outside of which may demons mass and hiss and gnash their terrible teeth til the cows come home, because we're inside, warm, Kings X. Stuart says he liked it best when Roger took a guitar solo. His eyes would roll up under his closed lids and you could tell he was gone, man, gone. *Those* were the days. Stuart doesn't say so, but we can tell.

There's a man with a beer gut setting up. He's chain-smoking, impatient, fussing with the equipment. "Who's that guy," I ask. "That's Roger Howse," Stuart says, "that's my man." Roger Howse may be terrific but he sure can't be big. He's both headliner and roadie. As far as he's concerned, the first set stinks. He isn't hearing what he wants. He's pissed off. He keeps fiddling with the amp. He sure can play the blues, and sing it too – Stuart was right – but let him leave that amp alone, let him go inside himself. I like the look of that Sean Harris. I recognize him from El Viento Flamenco. Roger Howse likes his looks too. Sean Harris brings in a new amp for the second set and the new amp works perfectly. Roger Howse beams and Sean Harris beams, and set two is all the blues. Jesus, set two is the blues itself. The first time Roger's eyes roll up under his lids we turn around to smile at Stuart and his eyes are full of tears. Ah, Stuart. *These* are the days too. They have to be. We didn't know you, we didn't know you and Janet back then.

33

THE ROSE AND THISTLE

There's a dead cat hangin on the line

The air in this bar is blue. You're a smoker by default. The performers can't wait for the break. They'll all sit down at the table nearest the window and light up. If someone turned the lights on you'd see the smoke hanging thick as a fog rolled in through The Narrows. Your clothes are soaking it up. They already smell of your time alone here, listening to this English Department reggae and waiting for Ben to join you when he's caught up. Just to sit and quietly talk a little for a damn change. Pour a little something on your melancholy. Hope it doesn't get out of control. You don't want to be climbing Prescott with red eyes again. You can explain smoke but not tears. Ah, but this town is too small. This town you love is too fucking small, or else Jack and Bev would not be walking in right now and paying their four bucks and coming over to join you. Which means that Ben will not. His sick smile behind the bar is telling you that. And here you go. Here goes another night of jolly pretend. And it's not angels hovering up Prescott and past Rawlins Cross, it's not angels waiting on Monkstown Road. It's not. Nobody's going to be flying away tonight. There's a brand new kitchen to hear all about. That's what there is, that's *all* there is for you tonight. Better face up to that and pay attention. Better squash your little middle class grief and fucking get on with it.

THE BLARNEY STONE

I don't care what Mr Crump don't allow
I'm gonna barrelhouse anyhow

When Folk Club was at The Blarney Stone we sometimes walked down without knowing who was on. Open mike is often the best part anyhow. That's how we found Terri-Lynn Eddy in full cry. "Santa Claus Blues." Was it December? Who cares. Give me that big raw voice wrapped around "Santa Claus Blues" any time of year. It was the first and last time I saw every single patron in The Blarney Stone shut up and listen. Even the musicians at Folk Club are talkers, you see, so most of the time you could drop an anvil in there and nobody'd notice. It's a mystery to me why performers don't slit their wrists after some of these gigs. But on this night nobody was even playing the VLTs. "She's only fifteen," I heard somebody say. Is that possible? A fifteen-year-old Mama from around the Bay holding everybody in this bar in the palm of her hand. Half a dozen girlfriends were with her, crowded around a table a few feet from the stage, which is just a low riser in front of a bay window. The friends came into their own when Terri-Lynn ran out of encores. That's something else I never saw at Folk Club, not before or since – an encore. "She Taught Me How to Yodel," one yelled. "I'm not going to *yo*del," spat Terri-Lynn, and there was the kid behind the woman belting out that raunch. How did she get a bye into the blues? I sure hope it wasn't coming out of her life. Well, she was no Wilf Carter, but she could yodel. As the song began, one of the friends suddenly flicked on a lighter and started to wave it back and forth like at the big concerts and another friend quickly suppressed her. "Santa Claus Blues" one more time, then the door prize draw, the break, and a set of traditional jigs and reels and polkas with button accordion, fiddle, bohdran and guitar.

Now it's two years later, and Terri-Lynn has been discovered. There are posters for the Terri-Lynn Eddy Band all over town. Close-up on her face with sultry eyes looking out over dark glasses. Well, she wasn't going to stay fifteen, and it's none of my damn business anyway. I just hope she's still wailing for the love of it.

JOHNNY BURKE'S

Don't drink a black cow's milk
Don't you eat a black hen's egg

In 'nonlecture I,' e.e. cummings makes his audience "a strictly egocentric proposition." He means to speak about himself, as Harvard University asked him to, but first he pauses, having led his listeners perfectly, and then he hits them with this: "who, if I may be so inconsiderate as to ask, isn't egocentric? Half a century of time and several continents of space, in addition to a healthily developed curiosity, haven't yet enabled me to locate a single peripherally-situated ego." Surprised laughter. You can hear laughter on the tape, but not the tears of sorrow and pleasure mixed, as cummings lovingly tells of his courageous mother's car accident – all that glass in her head and still thinking of others first – the collision that killed his father, "than whom no father on earth ever loved or ever will love his son more profoundly."

But I digress. That's the way I am. Rather than look at you and talk to you I jump away into the words of others, those distances I love. It keeps me standing still in the very socks and shoes I told you about. For all the good it did either of us. Stock still in this particular miserable cypher, this circumference of a dot.

GREEN SLEEVES

Black snake hangin round my door

"Ugh, there's a nasty leech. I'm not sitting out here! It's a leech, all right. Look there. They suck your blood."
"They do?"
"Damn right they do. I'm not sitting out here ever again!"

(Patron misidentifies slug)

FINNIGAN'S WAKE

Bring me a pillow for my poor head
A hammer to knock out my brains

He has already broken off in the middle of a song, left the room, returned, started up – impressive – precisely where he quit. Our table is a few feet from the mike, so when he starts to cough and choke again he can easily step out, grab my pint and take a couple of gulps. Without a by-your-leave. Well, it may be my beer, but his need is greater. Throat trouble is the least of what he's up against. The whole Liberal caucus is in the room behind him. They've had a pleasant Liberal dinner downstairs at NaGeira's and they've all come up here for after-dinner drinks and a smoke. There's no cover for restaurant customers – a good way to clear out lingering diners but a poor way to gather an audience. The caucus is raucous. Singer? What singer? The one who's been glancing at them with blue murder in his eye. If he hadn't met the gaze of Chuck Furey, Minister of Culture and Tourism, paying what attention he could, we might have had the spectacle of one of the world's best singer-songwriters losing it, running amok in a room full of elected philistines. But a spectacle is to watch, and we wouldn't have watched that. The unofficial Ron Hynes fan club would have risen as one and charged the other room.

But there is no rising. Even with another glug of my beer, Ron can't finish the set, breaks early.

We know his marriage is on the rocks, we know about the drugs. "My professional life is skyrocketing," he said to Kathleen Lippa of *The Express*; "my personal life's a mess. I'm a handful – a dangerous entity in the world. Have nothing to do with me." Big smile. But there've been no smiles tonight; his professional life is nosediving. So where's he going with his guitar? Where can he possibly go and what can he possibly do to recover after that?

FINNIGAN'S WAKE II

After all my hard travellin
Things about comin my way

"It's a profession full of pitfalls. And you need personal power to survive inside of it. And lots of it. On a daily basis. That's the only way to survive in this business. Nobody else can save you. You have to save yourself. Every day. *Every* day." That was in the interview too. Here's another version: after thirty years in the profession, his ego crushed so often it's past anthracite to diamond, Ron Hynes could cut glass. Of *course* he's coming back out to face the demons of indifference.

Mind you, it's not the same bar. The Liberal ranks are thinner. A big crowd of music lovers, Anita Best among them, has hustled over after the Ben Hepner concert. Anita's in charge of the Bards and Ballads series and invited Ron for this gig. Has she heard about the first set disaster or is she merely reading this crowd? Maybe she just wants to hear "Tickle Cove Pond." Anyway, after his first song a new one not yet a winner with the audience, Anita has a word with Ron. "Tickle Cove Pond" is exactly right. It even snags a couple of Liberals. They swing their chairs around and sing the chorus with the rest of us. Then "Old Brown's Daughter," then "Sonny's Dream." Now everyone is hooked. The bar fills with our voices:

> Still got my high school jacket
> Still got my high school ring
> Tucked in a corner of my wallet
> Is a tattered photo of The King
> > Yet I have to cry
> > Starin' back at silent eyes
> > I saw a star burn out last night
> > South of Cryer's paradise

Barb – she plays violin with the St. John's Symphony Orchestra – leans over and speaks into my ear: "Ben Hepner was great, but this is better." Ron's in the groove and we're in it with him, now belting out the chorus of that beautiful nonsense written for his daughter:

> Who's the bestest baby
> in the whole whirly-perleedies?
> The whole whirly-perl

Whole whirly-perl
Whole whirly-perleedies
Whirly-perleedies

That woman by the bar – I must learn her name because her face always shows the transport I feel myself when Ron Hynes and his listeners meet exactly halfway. *These* are the days, *this* is where it's at, and we know it. The city has grown and grown tonight. Right now it's the one we'd choose – no question – the very one we'd choose over any other city in the whole wide

whirly-perleedies.

Mp [pomt bptuj pf is s;pggomg tjrpigj tje fdrozz;e after c;psomg to,e. – dpwm

What's with these sound systems? This one will not adjust to Jim Joyce's satisfaction. It's going to be another long night for the performer. Not a disaster this time (and no sudden rising of the corpse), just a kind of hot-lead-seeping-into-the-marrow sort of heaviness, I'd say. Though maybe it's just me, antennae quivering, picking this up and laying it down on Mr. Joyce – *James* Joyce on the posters and his CD. Stuart and Janet brought me down to hear him. He has already played "Kansas City" for Stuart – catcalls from the Irish patrons of this Irish bar – who starts for Kansas tomorrow. For research, not one of those pretty little women. In the second set, Jim will play "Flower of Scotland," and Stuart's eyes will leak, his arms wave about in heartfelt parody of Scots national fervour. Stuart being of the Seattle Piersons.

James Joyce. The name makes me shiver, though of course this is not the mole-sighted literary giant. It's the Irish tenor of the same name, now dividing his time between Florida and Goose Bay. He's in demand in Florida bars, and he likes the golf down there, but his wife has been transferred to Labrador. How does he like Goose Bay? Well…the hiking is great.

Not an outright disaster. But yesterday was Flip Janes' funeral and the whole arts community is way down. I saw Jim's shoulders shaking during the service. And the sound muddy tonight. And the lead singer for Shanneyganock stepping onto the stage just like he owned it and fiddling with the sound board. Then weaseling his way into an invitation to do a couple of songs in that rich Stan Rogers baritone and the audience loving him. And me confessing that I break 80 once in a long while, while Jim's best so far is 86. All of which probably amounts to nothing but me laying my weight on him. You can lift the world if that little interior gyroscope is whirling true, but I sense a wobbling. Maybe it takes one to know one.

One time, Janet says, it was late. She and Stuart were about to leave the Joyces' house when Jim thought of a song. So he got out the guitar and, four hours later… Stuart is full of wonder: how can any one person store up all that music? Where does an Irish tenor reach inside himself to pull out "Kansas City" when he hasn't sung it in a decade? Stuart himself can remember a half dozen songs, and one is "They're Moving Father's Grave to Build a Sewer."

Those wonderful tenor pipes and all that music – you want it lining the heart or the soul or the pit of the stomach, whatever it is the demons go for. If he has demons. If they aren't all mine. No point both of us slogging through the drizzle after last call, down Water to George Street, up George past all those Guinness-Book-of-Records bars – a bad mistake, when you're already down, to drift like a cypher past all that pulsing life – back to New Gower, Duckworth, up Prescott home. No point the both of us being solitary in the bosom of our families.

THE SHIP INN

You never miss the water
Til your well run dry

You had your night music. Been and gone. The honey sweetened your tongues and there was nobody watching, least of all yourselves. Everything sweet and slick in the honey moon. You will never, *never* slide like that again. You want to seal it all up in amber, all you lost the second you lay down out there. Habit already creeping on you when you rose.

But won't the honey moon slide around next month?

Who told you that? Moon doesn't move. You turn around her.

Go back outdoors. Don't say "velvet meniscus," don't give me "engorged with its population of the night." Just drop your tone way down and go back out. There's something bright and slick across the curve of that dark pool. Go back and lay your cheek down there. Lay yourself down and take a look.

It's not the same, is it? It's all changed. What did you expect?

BLUES FOR THE BLUES

Jannie Edwards

Even the blind man knows
When he's walking in the sun
—B.B. King

What I would give
What I would give
for a horn
in this lonely room

Give to get pulled
through the blue marrow of a climbing slide
pitch its arc
perfectly
to your absence

What I would give to play the note that pulls
you all the way in
To do for you what red
does for blue
Go deeper

Man, what I would give
for you

So long gone
from this lonesome bed
hot
with the midnight blues

ST. MARY BLUES

Patrick Friesen

I'm sitting here on a dime
watching the trains slide away
sitting here on a dime
watching the trains slide away
there's nowhere else I'd rather stay
than st. mary at the dying of the day

snow sifting cross the tracks
sun dogs howling round the moon
I'm going nowhere fast
guess I won't be gone too soon

don't want to ride a limo
don't want to ride a hearse
don't mind where I'm going
long as I don't get there first

and I'm sitting here on a dime
watching black cat slipping through
sitting here on a dime
watching black cat slipping through
there's nothing else I'd rather do
than tune these strings and sing the st. mary blues

st. mary blues
st. mary blues
lady's making angels in the snow
and I know it's time to blow

I'm sitting here on a dime
watching the trains slide away
I'm sitting here on a dime
watching the trains slide away
there's nowhere else I'd rather stay
than st. mary at the dying of the day

oh I've got lots of friends
just lying back in their tombs
they don't have much to say
but they sure got lots of room

don't want to ride a limo
don't want to ride a hearse
don't mind where I'm going
long as I don't get there first

I'm sitting here on a dime
watching black cat slipping through
sitting here on a dime
watching black cat slipping through
there's nothing else I'd rather do
than tune these strings and sing the st. mary blues

st. mary blues
st. mary blues
lady's making angels in the snow
and I know it's time for me to blow

WAITING FOR
ROBERT JOHNSON

Sue Goyette

This is an opened bottle of whiskey, the seal
already broken
and this is a drunk man, not caring
who he'd been flirting with,
the Mr. So and So she called out to
over her husband's shoulder. This is the wooden table
between the men and this is the poison
the man drank without knowing, never taking his eyes off her
as the whiskey fuel-lined down his throat.
This is the match that lit the fuel and this is pneumonia
in August, the blues and the woman
who had to go home with her husband.
These are the marks she made on his back
with her nails, this is his back and these are the marks
his wife made as she cried out. This is the man's face
in the pillow, stifling his cries until he is finished. This is his wife's eyes
looking at the bedpost, looking at the ceiling, at her nails.
Anywhere. This is their bed, this is the husband
fucking the blues, her face shadowed and absent, her man
dead, his guitar buried and her husband's body
lying the length of her. And this is her not being able to
move, barely able to breathe. She is lonelier than the guitar, her neck,
and oh, her frets. This is a woman who wants to be haunted,
who will spend the rest of her days feeling hopeful when the curtain
moves and the window is closed. This is a woman in love
with a man who has become a falling spoon or a shadow
on the wall. She will learn to touch herself with his hands,
his tongue, slide guitar and steel strings. She will tune each day
until her fingers callous and her throat is raw
from trying. This is her porch, her geraniums,
the screen door she never locks because she knows the songs now,
she knows the way they always end up wanting to come right back
home. This is a woman who'll always wait
for a man who'll never come back.
This is the waiting
and this is the never
coming back.

SELF-SUFFICIENT BLUES

Maureen Hynes

Workin girl, I wake up every day
with the wanna-stay-in-beds
Workin girl, I wake up every day
fix my house instead.

Got the self-sufficient blues, got them down fine.
Got the self-sufficient blues, just me, myself and mine.
It's the fix my own plumbing, tie my own shoes,
make my own decisions, paint my own blues.

Got my education, got my medication,
got my job down pat.
Got my education, got my medication,
got a therapist and a cat.

Got the half a head of lettuce, the salad greens go bad.
Got the full fridge, empty table, one wineglass sads.
Got the self-sufficient blues, the flying solo crime
Goin through the motions and I'm getting by just fine.

But what's missing is some kissing,
a pair of boots inside my door.
What's missing is some kissing
a little laughin' and l'amour.

Got the self-sufficient blues, got the me, myself and mine.
Got the self sufficient blues, oh I carry on just fine.

TATTOOS & CIGARETTES

Mark Jarman

Taxis come and taxis go, junkies speak of Angelo
taxis come and taxis go, junkies ask for Angelo
and I'm just mowing my lawn
I'm just washing my car

I find needles on the road
my boy eats his Cheerios
Find a needle on the road
my boy eats his Cheerios
And I'm just mowing my lawn
I'm just washing my car

Shopping cart in their yard
shopping cart in their yard
they got the junkie walk
they got the junkie talk
and I'm just mowing my lawn
I'm just washing my car

Tattoos and cigarettes
tattoos and cigarettes
lay the money on a bed
lose the money on a bet
and I'm just mowing my lawn
I'm just washing my car

DR. DOOM CATHOLIC BLUES   *Gillian Jerome*

Blue rinse in the bible club
since I been born.

Money basket jingle bells
since I been born.

Eyes on them choir girls
since I been born.

Guilty so guilty
since I been born.

Hot-box in the tabernacle
since I been born.

Holy water hail storm
since I been born.

Blackstrap chapel gong
since I been born.

Mercy oh mercy
since I been born.

Nailpolish knee-highs on
since I been born.

Father Tom's telethon
since I been born.

Lordy oh Lordy
since I been born.

to Trallee

love Michael

TRIANGLE BLUES

Michael Kenyon

My baby run off with another man but she aint runnin fast.
She runnin with a new man but she keeps runnin back.
Cant tell if we're goin or comin and that is a fact.

I drive her to the airport and pick her up from there.
Said I drive her to the airport and pick her up from there.
She been with him, been with him, new ribbons in her hair.

She is a lost angel baby, a sad thing to see.
She is my lost angel baby and a sad thing to see.
When she gets a bit stronger I might cut her free.

EGGPLANT

Michael Kenyon

Bought me an eggplant big as a bruise,
tapped it for ripeness, it gave me the news.
Said you're dead, baby, baby you're dead,
if you was alive you'd be singing the blues.

Found me a woman with a heart on her sleeve.
Said whose is that, honey, whose heart on your sleeve?
Said you're dead, baby, baby you're dead.
If you was alive you'd know who to grieve.

Hey where you going with that bruise?
Where you going with that old bruise?
You're surely dead, baby, been and gone dead,
you don't need no bloodclot, don't need no fuse.

Well I got nothing to say and nothing to say,
I got nothing to say and nothing to say.
Must be dead, baby, must be I'm dead.
If I was alive I'd get down and pray.

DASHBOARD MARY

Ryan Knighton

Ready dashboard mary on a nicotine fuse
blazin Jeremiah 8 track bullfrog blues
I earned a Sally Jesse jaundice for my fidelity runs
& lost a trailer park pad soakin' Kingdom Come

Been punchdrunk lonesome on assembly line drift
diggin' punchclock dirt for the graveyard shifts
packin' perfume bombs for your bathtub blessings
so's bridegroom gumshoes smell a way to the wedding

But Lady Luck jacked the trailer & she drove herself north
bad luck be a lady boostin' all that I'm worth
she's from ground zero get go spittin' diamonds & toads
now the only thing between us is that Wonderbread Road

Down Wonderbread Road
that's where Lady Luck stole
no I ain't got a chance with her
& can't find my way home
I'm scratchin' eight
ballin' down Wonderbread Road

Waited Coquihalla long in the dumptruck hours
wantin' cul-de-sac hangtime picket fence flowers
plantin' red mojo roosters in the yellowing grasses
they grew flamingo jingles & her U-turn passes

Once a jitterbug bozo in a back seat rodeo
lazy-boy lovin' the recliners goin' down slow
but that's Xerox powder tarrin' Where You At Lane
just a thumb leafin' filthy through its coupon book days

Lady Luck she jacked the trailer & she drove herself north
bad luck is a lady boosted all that I'm worth
she's from ground zero get go spittin' diamonds & toads
now the only love between us is that Wonderbread Road

53

Down Wonderbread Road
that's where I'll go
I once had a chance
but crapped out on my throw
my luck she pulled up stakes
for that Wonderbread Road

Now I'm Chevy Nova fueled chompin' gear tooth ready
gonna bust that hog wild goin' yellow line steady
not a fastfood possum playin' chickenshit soul
but a Leadbelly foot floorin' Midas touch gold

Down Wonderbread Road
just you watch me go
all bets are off
I gotta win, place or show
I'm gonna pass Lady Luck by
on that Wonderbread Road
gonna pass Lady Luck up
for that Wonderbread Road

DRY LAND BLUES

I have walked the slippery slope
on the backbone of a whale – top
that if you will, with remedies
for erectus, and gramercies.

> There's a cold wind blowing.
> Keep your head in your hat.

Knew this woman more than human,
she as grim as her own rhyme.
Turned she into ghost a feller.
Gave a grin a quite a pallor.

> There's a dry wind blowing.
> It's blowing straight at me.

Instant love comes in a package
packed in Spanish fly and wreckage.
Knew this man who learned to bray.
Hope to hell he were not me.

BLUES FOR NO ONE

Patrick Lane

You had the last word, hello is what you said,
how was I to know you meant goodbye.
Now I'm drinking whiskey in this Last Call bar I've found
and you're not here to drink another round.

Refrain:

>   Snow keeps on whispering, whiskey never cries.
>   A barroom window's always closed and nobody can fly.
>   Snow keeps on drifting, nobody knows why.
>   Women are the wounds you hold when something in you dies.

I think you hurt your dreaming back when you were just a girl.
I don't know why and now I'll never know.
Each guy who buys you whiskeys wants a piece of your sad bones.
You know that cause it's what you've always known.

I don't know why I loved you, guess that love is mostly cold,
it's how I feel now that I'm feeling old.
There's just one name for wishing, there's a hundred for the snow.
They all blow on the highway drifting slow.

A woman's sometimes lonely, sometimes never there at all.
The whiskey and cocaine's your only song.
If I ever tried to find you I would look behind my mind.
It's where you stayed when all of you was gone.

Nowhere's half of someone, half of what I called your heart.
It changed like wind is what you used to say.
Your name hurts in this whiskey, it's a needle in the snow
I'd look for it if I thought you'd ever stay.

No one knows the leaving of a woman when she's gone,
no one looks for steps in drifting snow.
Looking's mostly lonely, just another lonely song.
Call it what you want, then call it gone.

THAT DIRT ROAD

Ross Leckie

I would prefer not to go down
       that dirt road without my
little red wagon. My battered tin
       lunch pail says I have somewhere
to go, but I don't want to go down
       that dirt road without my
protractor set, you know, and my
       compass. I'm going down, and crying
can't make me stay in this
       alfalfa, I'm going down that
dirt road. I would prefer not.
       To go down that dirt road without
my pink chewable eraser and its
       sumptuous rubbery soya curd
dryness would be so naked and you know
       I would prefer not to go down
that dirt road without my Huckleberry
       Hound t-shirt. The buttercups
that grow by the ditch don't go down
       that dirt road. They hold fast
where they're soiled. The forsythia
       by the corner of the veranda doesn't
go down. It rockets up in a golden sting
       of flowers careening into holiday
fireworks. The forget-me-nots and heal-all
       don't go down that dirt road.
I would prefer not to go down that dirt road.

WOKE UP THIS MORNING

Ross Leckie

Tell me, Mr Sol, where you were last night.
The west wind curled the leaves of corn.
The field mice scuttled through the stalks.
The malignant cows coughed in the barn.
The dog clicked across the linoleum floor.
The moths spun cotton around the yellow light.
The crickets scratched their hind-leg ache.
The maples stretched their limbs in a hush.
The sky bristled its hair like a cat.
The moon crusted the house in its chemical white.
I woke up this morning
and your clothes weren't fitting you right.

1

      How
hooked I –
      honey how

      hooked &
horny; hooked and happy-go-
             honking – hey, how

      hooked on your
honey-sweet honey I
      am.

2

Home-spooked
hotline.   Nobody's li'l number

one.   Big-eyed
radium child on stretched-out scrims of alert –

you could go off in *my*
life?…Well of

all

things!

3

Hot po-
tato momma, got you in my

mouth all night.
Absenty

lady –
land o'

livin, I could pay my
rent all year & *still* owe dues.

4

Some kinda
stunts & wonders? Hocus-
focus? Hot cross

nerve ends?
Come on c'mon nice
lady, we ain't got all

lifetime!…Indefatigably-adored one:

please to
appear on the sheet right now, called up by
succulent, shrink-wrapped, wholly-refundable me.

5

Wal, acey deucey
        trey divide –
I'm a guy
        with a fine wide-eyed

lady freckles too &
        squirms when she
feels good, I feel so
        good just

doin aw
        shucks
tricks an she's
        SOFISTIKATED!

6

Hey honey,
        it
sizzles.

Come closer, wanna
        see your
eyeballs roll!

Wanna
        tell ya
things…

Don't like it, just
        don't come
in here – y'

        hear?

GENUINE IMITATION AMERICAN EUROPEAN HOMESICK BLUES

Slava Lurpil

You always try to make me do things I don't wanna do,
I'm always sick and tired – and now I'm sick and tired of you.

Ya, you're the fishhead in my soup,
Ya, you're the bad milk in my tea,
I look at you and want to move
myself to Tennessee.

I'm bored, and that's a bad sign –
but I've been bored since I began to crawl.

You're like a Ford whose brakes are gone,
you've rolled downhill and got me pinned against the wall.

Ya, but if I didn't have a Ford truck, wouldn't have no truck at all.

TOBACCO BELT

Rick Maddocks

Daddy wore his tobacco belt
Strapped to his waist like a beaver pelt or something
He said son don't set your expectations high
And you won't get disappointed
Well I had nothing to do
And I had nothing to say
And he don't know how I felt
He don't know how I felt
Strapped in, buckled down in this tobacco belt

Broken bottles down in the ditch
Tore this tobacco belt stitch by stitch
Smoke so thick that I could barely breathe
Lord knows I did my best to up and leave
I had nothing to do
And I had nothing to – you said it not me
But it's easy hating everyone
When you know that you're the stranger
Now folks round here either got death up their sleeves
Or basements full of danger
And they don't know how I felt
They don't know how I felt
Strapped in buckled down, booted around
Shot down, pissed on in this tobacco belt

He ain't gonna punch another hole in his tobacco belt
Cos when the truth hits it wells up like a welt
I guess I knew that the die was cracked
The first time daddy's belt split my back
Now he's got nothing to do
And he's got nothing to say
But now he knows how I felt
Now he knows how I felt
Strapped in, buckled down, booted around town
Laughed at, shot down, pissed on
Get out while I'm still young from this tobacco belt

63

SUBTERRANEAN
RED HOT NEWFOUNDLAND
CODFISH BLUES

David W. McFadden

Well I dreamed ya gone fishing but yer still out waddering da lawn.
Yeah, I dreamed ya gone fishing but yer still out waddering da lawn.
Ya been waddering fer hours, but dem fish by now is long gone.

Y'has to dig for yer worms, you just can't wadder da grass.
Y'has to dig for yer worms, you just can't wadder da grass.
When dey sees what yer doing dey'll go back down real fast.

You gets up at noon and y'reaches fer a cold Moosehead.
Yeah, you gets up at noon and y'reaches fer a cold Moosehead.
You keeps dis up, soon you be no bedder dan dead.

I loves ya baby, I loves it when you comes home wif fish.
Yep, I loves ya baby, I loves it when you comes home wif fish.
But tonight you gonna be eating a real cold dish.

Well I dreamt ya gone fishing but yer still out waddering da plants.
Yeah, I dreamt ya gone fishing but yer still out waddering da plants.
Keep on yer waddering cuz I'm heading home to Come By Chance.

LONG SAULT BLUES

Well I don't know where that Long Sault's got to
It's just dry bone all the time
Yes I don't know where that Long Sault's got to
and it's dull as that dry bone bottom all the time
And I'm waiting here with his unemployment cheque Charlie
For that long gone Long Sault man of mine.

Well they took me down to the river
And they showed me a heap of bones
Yes they took me down to the dried up river
And they showed me these bald old stones
Said that is all he ever was goodbye forget him
You're better off just living on your own.

So I'm standing by the highway
With my suitcase by my side
Yes I'm standing on the 401 highway
And I'm thinking suicide
   (what *kind* suicide?
    Long Suicide)
And I don't care where you're going to mister
Cause there's something here that's died.

But then I heard he was up north in Kapuskasing
With his big gold saxophone
Yes I heard he was in a bar in Kapuskasing
Makin that same old sort of chucklin moan
And yes they said that he was chasing
Every piece of tail around for sale or loan.

Well when I heard that powerful news
I just broke down and cried
And when I moaned and sung the blues
It lit my fire inside
Now I'm going to find that Long Sault man
No matter where he hides.

And when I catch that man again
I'm going to fetch my crock of dandelion wine
Yes when that son of a bitch shows up again
We're going to sit and drink that 15 gallon crock of dandelion wine
Cause there's moves that he knows Charlie
You just can't buy in the five and dime.

BITCHIN B.C. BURSA BLUES

Don McKay

When your joints commence to rust
in that drizzlin B.C. damp
and you fall to cursin bursa
as your hips begin to clamp
when your left hip's sayin creak
and your right hip's sayin croak
and the clock says 3 a.m., you know
this isn't any joke
                      you got those
tragic bitchin B.C. bursa blues.

When you're headed for the kitchen
with those bum hips on your brain
3:15 and they're still twitchin
and you're walkin like John Wayne

                                in pain, you got

those tragic bitchin B.C. bursa blues.

Ibuprofen, Ibuprofen
o my Saint Glucosamine
strap those ice packs on like six guns
rub that old Witch Hazel Cream
Acupuncture, acupuncture
till I look like porcupine
gonna irrigate my aura
with some Okanagan wine
Think I'll get myself a shrink
who can re-arrange my head
gonna learn that Tai Chi cha cha
think I'll get my Tarot read
gonna rolf my inner child
gonna cone my inner ear
gonna dance the Jin Shin Do
till that bitchin disappears
then I'll get some Deep Massage
from some not-too-deep masseuse
                            and lose

these tragic B.C. bitchin bursa blues.

Got a nine dollar bill
          baby can you make me change
Got a nine dollar bill baby
          Baby can you make me change
You need a nest egg
          that's something I can arrange

Give you what I got
          Want to put it in your purse
Give you all this here
          Put it right in your purse
But you too busy baby
          Don't want to muss your dress

Ain't no modern man baby
          to slip it in no bank machine
No modern man baby
          to slip it in your bank machine
Got to slide up to the wicket
          give it to that high school queen

Big money in my pocket
          burns a hole in my clothes
All this money honey
          burning holes in my clothes
You look so cool baby
          you could cure my economic woes

Give you what I saved
          baby it's investment time
Want to give you what I saved up
          baby it's investment time
Hear you tell me baby
          your money's coming 'long fine

Gonna take it baby
      to some savings and loan
Gonna take it somewhere baby
      some other savings and loan
Such a rich man honey
      just cannot hide it at home

My old guitar baby
      I pull the strings 'n' slap the hole
Old guitar baby
      pull the strings slap the hole
Get just what I want out
      but some things I can't control

DJANGO BLUES

Jane Southwell Munro

Gypsy at the river, fishing – broke fingers grab a trout.
Gypsy at the river, fishing – broke fingers grab a trout.
Can't find him cause he's playing on his own.
Can't find him cause he's playing on his own.
He's catching time – eating them fine bones.

Tambourine girl whirling – feet fish flirting
with the ripple of a creek.
Tambourine girl whirling-feet fish flirting
with the ripple of a creek.
Can't see her cause she's circling on her own.
Can't see her cause she's circling on her own.
She's catching time – shaking them fine bones.

Django played the river's tones and tides –
salt currents swinging.
Django played the river's tones and tides –
salt currents swinging.
Can't call him cause he's listening on his own.
Can't call him cause he's listening on his own.
He's catching time – surprising them fine bones.

EMPTY HOUSE BLUES

P.K. Page

My house is empty but I don' want no one here
My house is empty but I don' want no one here
My bed is empty and the friggin' fridge is bare
there ain't no scrap fer a starvin' cat in there
no scrap for this cat neither
no scrap for this ol' cat
this ol' grey rundown cat

O dearie dearie god O dearie god
My bed is empty like a empty parkin' lot
Ain't no one parkin' there, ain't no one parkin' there
The snow pile up in corners and the house cry out at night
Ain't no one hold me tight
No other cat in sight
To fight me, hold me tight

My heart is empty an' I don' want no one here
My heart is empty an' I don' want no one here
Is empty like a empty six-pack beer
Empty and I don' want no one here
Don't want no one here.
No one here.

HOME LOAN BLUES

Daria Patriarchus

Going out to Brampton,
Brampton here I come.
Going out to Brampton,
I said Brampton here I come.
They've got some relatively inexpensive townhouses there,
and I'm gonna get me one.

I might take a Go train,
I might take a regional bus.
I gotta see my banker, there's a lot we gotta discuss.

I'm going out to Brampton,
I said Brampton here I come.
They've got some relatively inexpensive townhouses there,
and I'm gonna get me one.

GRAVITY BLUES

Jay Ruzesky

You know I'm fallin' for you baby, like an apple from a tree.
You know I'm fallin' for you baby, but you fly away from me.
I'm in orbit 'round you baby, so fast that I can't stand,
I just go around in circles, there's no place I can land.
I got the gravity blues and you know they always bring me down.

I seen you with another man, hangin' off of his long arms,
I seen you with another man, you know that does me harm.
You don't care about me baby, don't matter if I crash,
and I have to tell you somethin' girl, I'm runnin' out of gas.
(I'm gonna burn up.)
I got the gravity blues and you know they always bring me down.

Mr. Newton taught us somethin' 'bout the force of love,
saw how apples on the branches were swingin' up above.
Now apples pull to apples, simple as can be,
but must be I'm an orange 'cause you ain't drawn to me.
I got the gravity blues and you know they always bring me down.

(Mr. Newton, you have no idea.)

73

YOU DON'T KNOW NOTHING ABOUT BEING

David Seymour

When you hear me knock, let me come, and I'll come
laughing. Thought of laying you down all day,
but your feet were so damn cold in bed
didn't make me want to stay.

Your love ain't never gonna be for free.
Cruel honey-pie, you don't know nothing about being
and I wish you knew somethin',
cause you don't know nothing about being, anywhere with me.

I've known the space beside your body
know the words that can make you cry:
please don't hold me under that rain again
and ask me to harvest the sky.

Cruel honey-pie, you don't know nothing about being
and I wish you knew somethin',
cause you don't know nothing about being
anywhere with me.

Gonna wander the streets with a lamp and my heart
gonna fight for your love in the bars
you shone so bright, you cut me swiftly,
and now my life's the scar.

Cruel honey-pie, you don't know nothing about being
and I wish you knew somethin',
cause you don't know nothing about being
anywhere with me.

I've been lost before but never felt so broke,
even knocked at your door, but the lights were low.
Used to say the world's a sad place,
now I think it's true.
                    Just wanted you to know.

Cruel honey-pie, you don't know nothing about being
and I wish you knew somethin',
cause you don't know nothing about being
anywhere with me.

VIRGINIA WOOLF
SINGS THE BLUES

Sue Sinclair

My mama was the sweetest sugar cane
Yes, my mama was sweetest sugar cane
Ripe an' pure, my mama, freshest rain

She made the angels all cry out for shame
Listen to them angels all cryin' out for shame
My mama was made just as pretty as they came

I watched her put them pearls of hers around her lily throat
Yes, I watched her put them pearls right around her lily throat
An' sail off down the staircase, glidin' out, a driftin' boat

Shinin' at the table like the Lord he loved her best
She was shinin' at the table like the Lord he loved her best
Servin' up the roast, guests lookin' jealous at the rest

The Lord he got tired of hearin' them angels weep
He got tired, Lord, of watchin' an' hearin' angels weep
You know what you did, Lord – now I can't hardly sleep

Listen can you hear her, still singin', full of charm?
Listen can you hear her, still singin', full of charm?
I can almost see her dancin', skirts looped up on her arm

The doorbell hardly rings no more, no parties, fancy dress
The doorbell hardly rings no more, no parties, fancy dress
My papa's always angry, my sissy's in distress

He's a mean ol' snake, my papa, selfish as can be
He's a mean ol' snake, my papa, selfish as can be
He wore out poor young mama, and now he's tryin' me

I got the blues so bad, I don't know what to do
I got the blues so bad, I don't know what to do
Had a dream last night – deep river, darkest blue

COVER GIRL BLUES

Sue Sinclair

Been waitin' a long time, page twenty-three
Been waitin' a long time, page twenty-three
Looks like there's nothing happenin' for me

So it's the blues, boys, play 'em slow
So it's the blues, boys, play 'em real slow
Ain't nowhere but those blues to go

Castin' my eyes over my bare shoulder
Castin' my eyes over my bare shoulder
Waitin' for a ride but the page gets turned over

Now it's the blues, boys, play 'em slow
Now it's the blues, boys, keep playin' 'em slow
Ain't nowhere but those blues to go

Bloomingdale's bloomin', so what you gonna say?
Bloomingdale's bloomin', so what you gonna say?
Ain't no one else gonna see it your way

When the blues have got you, play 'em boys, so slow
When the blues have got you, play them blues slow
Ain't nowhere but those blues to go

I got colour if there ain't nothin' else I know
I got colour if there ain't nothin' else I know
Cheek bright red as cherry jelly roll

And it's the blues, boys, play 'em low
It's the blues, boys, you play 'em nice and now
Ain't nowhere but those blues to go

BLUES MY DADDY   *Adam Sol*
TAUGHT ME

Blues for Tommy Twostep
Blues for Einstein's Brain
Blues with No Mint Julep
Blues, I Missed My Plane

Cold Blues in a Snow Drift
Blues in Central Park
Blues for Moral Uplift
Blues Afraid of the Dark

I Left My Blues in Pittsburgh
I Can't Get This Blues Right
Blues for Eddie Ginsberg
Whose Momma Died Last Night

Blues for the Orangutan
Blues With Bloody Feet
My Uncle Was a Blues Man
Your Blues I'd Like to Meet

Blues That Fixed My Rifle
Blues in an Apple Core
Yeah, Sing this Blues My Wife
Will Kick Me to the Floor

Blues That Shines My Shoes
Blues for a Telethon
My Daddy Taught Me All My Blues
Blues, Where's My Daddy Gone?

LOW DOG DOWN

Karen Solie

March is like a landlord coming in, and it's never
ever going out again. There's a time for everything.
This isn't one of those. The clock fell off the wall
in 1984. Drop a cherry in it darling, pretty please.
The band sounds loose and queasy, like a terminal
disease. Our barmaid's name is Sheila. She's a natural
disaster. Her boyfriend's in the corner on his knees.
He wants to be a hole in the ground.

There's a hatchet in the kitchen
and the cook is on the lam. Lit out
with some whistle bait he picked up
off the drag. There are soldiers
in the harbour. Someone's ship
is going down. One more regular
bets the farm as if his luck
had turned around.

All the bluffers and the pointers and the cranks, crawl in
off the sidewalk with sugar in their tanks. We're all a little iffy,
eyeballing strangers on the side, hard-pressed to remember
our best lines on the fly. They couldn't be much worse if we
were paid. A tidy squeeze play in the corner means that someone's
got it made. There's trouble on the backlot. The cops
have broken ranks. In here, we've got the routine down in spades
digging us those holes in the ground.

It's the way the crow flies and this
godawful weather. The media,
small dogs, and rising prices
of tequila. It's assorted bonehead
bylaws. Unfinished business left
downtown. All those lousy deals
you've done as if your luck
had turned around.

You haven't ditched that sucker, he's still here, backed
into a corner by the skunkweed and the beer. He was exhausted
when you met him, now he's a rag out in the wind,
decked out retro Vegas with a shipment coming in. At last,
a little something we can use. Last call has pitched a highball
we aren't game to refuse. Saturday rolls over on us, coughs
it up, hits the bricks. Everybody wants to be your friend
and Sunday is a hole in the ground.

DECARIE'S ORCHARD

John Steffler

Well I'll be goin where Decarie's orchard was.
Wish I could fly. Goin where Decarie's orchard was.
Leave the station, cross the bridge, down the busy street,

there's one tree where the honey bees still buzz.
I know one tree where the honey bees still buzz.
Where she grows don't feel the city's heat.

Round the corner, through the gate, goodbye weariness,
found my happiness.
Her boughs bend down, her fruit is sharp and sweet.

Gonna pick her apples, let her branches rise.
Ease her load and let her branches rise.
I'm a lucky man, I landed on my feet.

Apples… smooth and sweet.
Decarie's orchard where it always was.
Springtime when my work's done I'm on that bus.

WHO'S CROOKED?

Since my baby left me,
I don't trust my sense of smell.

Since my baby left me,
I don't trust my sense of smell.

I thought those little trouts were sweet,
now I don't feel so well.

My sweet baby used to love me,
and when we were apart

she'd come to see me in my dreams
to tell me what was in her heart.

My baby used to love me,
then said her love for me had died,

and I've been four four four four years
without her at my side.

Now when she visits in my dreams
she's always sad and thin,

she seems to hope I'll touch her
and welcome her back in.

But when I telephoned her
just the other day

she said she wouldn't see me and
had nothing more to say.

Either I'm an ugly evil ugly
evil ugly evil guy

or for some crooked reason, that
crooked woman lied.

CRYING THE BLUES

Sharon Thesen

The fat red-haired woman, her deaf daughter, Bliss
all crying, and me

on my knees which looked
like crushed roses when I rose
from the rug   when I

rose from the rug all flushed and
sweaty   the blues

somewhere near my mind, our faces
all reflected in the door – myself, my acquaintance,
Bliss, her daughter, arms draped as comrades, tears

flowing, why

were we crying, I don't know but we'd just met
and I'd found out about the daughter
being deaf but could be it was existential

too.

DADA ANNA BLUE

Fred Wah

Oh lie me 27 in, Oh yes, do lie me
Do diner tick doe roll deer dust clear, ——Hear!
Oh, do go lightly don't
mind me twenty
seven sins and
likely let's have more.

Do dine her
squeeze her count her
her and
her, but where?

Do best do worst
lie spoonin' here
or ride the blinds
and night with her.
Do diner trick doe roll deer dust clear, ——Hear!
Lemon, yes, we're skin.

How are ya biscuit leaf
shakin' in the rust
jes' call red luck
You'll be another bloom.

Oh yes, oh yes, do lie me do.
Do diner tick doe roll deer dust clear, ——Hear!
On the line.

Press fresh Anna
put another on her hat
blue's to die for groans
so vocal yes to kiss her.
anna-nanna-nAH!

Nana Anna whom?
Do diner tick doe roll deer dust clear, ——Hear!
Dining on your name
before and after dinner.
You then You Yours truly I'm there.

Oh I know you know it Anna
honey dripper do salty rider
ANNA NANA BLUE
Do drop to here
I love your you yours!
Here and here and here.

NORTH WIND BLUES

Andy Weaver

Opened my door this mornin', north wind blowin' hard.
Opened my front door this mornin', north wind was blowin' hard.
Ravens overhead, crows cacklin' in my yard.

Sun got down so quick, it went away 'n ran
Yeah, yellow ol' sun got down so quick, turned its face 'n ran.
Moon grinnin' at me, north wind more'n I could stand.

Venus burnin' in the sky, she winked her eye at Mars.
Yeah, Venus burnin' up that sky, pitchin' woo at ol' man Mars.
North wind started groanin', scared off all the stars.

I closed my door this evenin', north wind blew real hard.
Closed my door this evenin', north wind was blowin' hard.
My old lady dealin' fortunes, she pulled out the blackest card.

MONTANA MOTEL BLUES   *Christopher Wiseman*

Big hot sun is slidin', drips like oil down through the sky.
That Montana sun is slidin', drips like oil down through the sky.
And I just can't get my thoughts right, no matter how I try.

The blues can mean you're broken, the blues can mean just sad.
You know the blues can mean you're broken or the blues can mean just sad.
But whatever blues I'm nursin', I ain't never felt this bad.

That old song has it right, motel ceiling stares you down.
I know that old song has it right, the motel ceiling stares you down.
I'm in a breeze-block prison in a nowhere breeze-block town.

Sheets smell kinda musty, towels are worn-out thin.
Yeah the sheets smell kinda musty, towels are worn-out thin.
Oh Lord don't I know it, it's just the state I'm in.

The blues can mean you're broken, the blues can mean just sad.
Yeah the blues can mean you're broken, the blues can mean just sad.
But whatever blues I'm nursin', I ain't never felt this bad.

Moon over Montana, its light is shinin' down.
This moon over Montana, its light comes pourin' down.
Gonna leave tomorrow, don't look for me around.

SCORCHED HEART BLUES

Robert Wooldridge

You drought the earth around me, drain me 'til I'm dry
My love has burned me to you, left me here to fry
You drought the earth around me, drain me 'til I'm dry
But until you melt me clean away, I'm burning 'til I die

You've got such a striking smile, girl
Like a match head bustin' out
Won't someone please come 'round
Come 'round and put me out

Now my feet are blazing, flames crawling up my sides
I'm at your door, I'm heating up, throwing sparks into the sky
Now my feet are blazing, flames crawling up my sides
So sear your love into my flesh, no need to cauterize

You've got such a striking smile, girl
Like a match head bustin' out
Won't someone please come 'round
Come 'round and put me out

And now my heart's on fire, babe, smoke coming out my eyes
Like lava you flow over me, as soon as I'm inside
And now my heart's on fire, babe, smoke coming out my eyes
But when you've got me down to embers, babe, what's left to crucify?

DEAD PALE PENIS
PERSON BLUES

Charles Wright

Woke up this morning,
               my dick was white and lean,
Woke up this morning,
               my dick was white and lean,
Well, you know, pretty mama,
               you know what that must mean.

I'm History's fool,
               you know I'm riptide bound,
Well, I'm History's fool,
               you know I'm riptide bound,
So look for me, pretty mama,
               look for me out and down.

Gone before my time,
               I'm all hogged down and tied,
Gone before my time,
               I'm all hogged down and tied,
So shamed and lorn, pretty mama,
               I like to up and died.

Charles Wright

It's Saturday afternoon at the edge of the world.
White pages lift in the wind and fall.
Dust threads, cut loose from the heart, float up and fall.
Something's off-key in my mind.
Whatever it is, it bothers me all the time.

It's hot, and the wind blows on what I have had to say.
I'm dancing a little dance.
The crows pick up a thermal that angles away from the sea.
I'm singing a little song.
Whatever it is, it bothers me all the time.

It's Saturday afternoon and the crows glide down,
Black pages that lift and fall.
The castor beans and the pepper plant trundle their weary heads.
Something's off-key and unkind.
Whatever it is, it bothers me all the time.

ONE WAY TRIP

Rachel Wyatt

Don't put your boots on, baby,
Take that look right off your face,
You can't follow where I'm going,
You can't come with me to this place.

Got this single ticket
For a one-way-only trip
And I'll tell you somethin', honey,
Ain't no space for you on this ship.

    So don't put your boots on, baby,
    Just don't put your sock feet in.
    Those big black boots o' yours, babe,
    Ain't nowhere for you to go.

When I left you last time
You come right after me,
Found me in a motel, saw
Somethin' you didn't oughta see.

But this time you can't follow,
Ain't no forwardin' address,
Ain't no map or bus stops,
Babe, you're never gonna guess.

    So don't put your boots on, baby,
    Just don't put your sock feet in.
    Those big black boots o' yours, babe,
    Ain't nowhere for you to go.

Yeah, don't put those boots on, honey,
I'll be right out of touch,
Or your leather jacket
Or the cap you like so much.

Don't put your boots on, baby,
It's a trip you don't wanna make.
Gonna leave you now, baby,
Right now, before I wake.

BROKE FIDDLE BLUES

Jan Zwicky

Got up this mornin,
　　　　rain pissin down like some monsoon,
Yeah, warm rain in January,
　　　　just like that old monsoon.
They say the climate's changin,
Babe, all my fiddle strings they outta tune.

Wise lady told me
　　　　folks got rhythm like the trees got leaves,
Wise lady told me
　　　　(don't you *worry,* girl!)
　　　　folks got rhythm just like trees got leaves.
Don't like this weather, mama,
Muzak never set me at my ease.

Went down to the seashore,
　　　　couldn't hear no rhythm in the waves,
Mmmm down at the seashore,
　　　　wasn't no rhythm in the waves.
Smart folk say meanin's dead,
They happy shoppin on its grave.

It happen to the jazz man,
　　　　he couldn't feel no difference between two & four,
Yeah, it happen to the jazz man
　　　　(happen to him first, baby)
　　　　couldn't feel no difference between two & four.
Happen to us all, babe, earth don't breathe
Won't be no music anymore.

Got up this mornin,
　　　　saw my fiddle broke to pieces on the floor,
Got up this mornin,
　　　　yeah, that fiddle, it was broke to pieces on the floor.
Leaves turnin yellow in the springtime,
Ain't no exit, baby, cause there ain't no door.

Ken Babstock was born in Newfoundland and grew up in the Ottawa Valley. He is the winner of the 2000 Atlantic Poetry Prize and the 2000 Milton Acorn Poetry Prize for his first collection of poems, *Mean*. His second collection, *Days into Flatspin*, appeared in spring 2001 from Anansi.

bill bissett: am based in toronto in vancouver a lot travl dewing readings and showing paintings wanting 2 keep on xploring all the media genres i can am devotee uv writing sound n image space

Shane Book was born in Peru and raised in Canada and Ghana. He is the recent recipient of a National Magazine Award and The *Malahat Review* Long Poem Prize as well as Southern Illinois University's Charles Johnson Award in Poetry and The Poetry Center's Rella Lossy Prize. In 1998, he was granted a *New York Times* Fellowship in Poetry to attend New York University, where he subsequently earned his MA. In the spring of 2001 he received a Teaching-Writing Fellowship from the Iowa Writers' Workshop where he is currently completing his MFA.

Adam Chiles' poetry has appeared in *The Malahat Review, The Fiddlehead, Prism International, Nimrod International, Event, Grain* and *Washington SQ*. He also appears in *Hammer and Tongs: A Smoking Lung Anthology*. He will be attending the University of Arizona this fall.

George Elliot Clarke be from Black Nova Scotia (Africadia). His latest books of poetry be *Execution Poems* (2001) and *Blue* (2001).

Lynn Coady is the author of *Strange Heaven*, a novel, *Play the Monster Blind*, a collection of stories, as well as an untitled novel coming out with Doubleday Canada in 2002. She also writes plays, essays, and reviews.

Brad Cran is the publisher of Smoking Lung Press and a contributing editor at *Geist* Magazine. His first book of poetry, *The Good Life*, will be published by Nightwood Editions in 2002.

Lorna Crozier has always wanted to be a country-blues singer. Since she can't stay in key she writes poetry and teaches at the University of Victoria. Her tenth book, *What the Living Won't Let Go*, received the Dorothy Livesay Award for poetry in 2000.

Lynn Davies lives in McLeod Hill, N.B. Her first collection of poems, *The Bridge that Carries the Road*, was published by Brick Books in 1999.

John Donlan is a poetry editor with Brick Books and a reference librarian at the Vancouver Public Library. His books of poetry are *Domestic Economy* (Brick Books, 1990, reprinted 1997), *Baysville* (House of Anansi, 1993), and *Green Man* (Ronsdale Press, 1999).

Barry Dempster is the author of seven books of poetry, as well as two collections of short stories, a children's book and a novel. He lives in Holland Landing, Ontario.

Adam Dickinson is a PhD student in English at the University of Alberta. His first book of poetry will be published by Brick Books in 2002. He lives and plays guitar in Edmonton.

Stan Dragland lives in St. John's, Newfoundland.

Jannie Edwards lives and writes in Edmonton where she also teaches at Grant MacEwan College. Her first book of poetry is *The Possibilities of Thirst*.

Patrick Friesen, a Manitoban by birth, teaches at Kwantlen University College in Vancouver. He writes poetry, songs, drama and texts for radio, dance and improvisational music. His most recent book is *Carrying the Shadow* (Beach Holme, 1999).

Sue Goyette's first book of poems, *The True Names of Birds* (Brick Books, 1998), was shortlisted for the Pat Lowther, the Gerald Lampert and the Governor General's Awards. Her first novel will be published in spring 2002 by HarperCollins.

Maureen Hynes is a Toronto poet whose first book, *Rough Skin*, won the Gerald Lampert Award. Her second book, *Harm's Way*, was published by Brick Books in 2001.

Mark Jarman, author of *19 Knives*, *New Orleans is Sinking* and *Salvage King Ya!*, teaches at the University of New Brunswick and is working on a non-fiction book about Ireland. He briefly played bass in a garage band.

Gillian Jerome is a heretic who lives and writes in the District of Damnation, Vancouver, B.C..

Michael Kenyon lives on North Pender Island. His most recent books are *Durable Tumblers*, a collection of stories, and *Broad Street Blues*, poems.

Ryan Knighton teaches literature and other writings at Capilano College where he also works as editor of *The Capilano Review*. His first collection of poetry, *Swing in the Hollow*, was published by Anvil Press (2001).

Robert Kroetsch is a prairie-born poet and novelist and a retired professor.

Patrick Lane's first influence was "Smokey White-Stocking and the Apple Valley Stompers," country blues of the forties. He writes poetry instead, not knowing how to play anything except his head.

Ross Leckie lives on the banks of the muddy Saint John, where he has been known to wail mournfully on his harps. These poems are dedicated to Lightnin' Hopkins. Blues in another key can be found in *The Authority of Roses* from Brick Books.

Dennis Lee was born and lives in Toronto.

The **Slava Lurpil** Circle consists of Kim Maltman, Roo Borson, Andy Patton, Janice Gurney and André Alexis. It is dedicated to the translation of the works of Slava Lurpil into English and works from rough glosses provided by the author.

Rick Maddocks' first book, *Sputnik Diner*, is a collection of linked novellas and stories published by Knopf Canada. It will be released by Vintage Canada in Spring 2002. He records and performs music in Vancouver with the Hands Collective. "Tobacco Belt," based on a short story by the same name, is sung as if through a prison's visiting-room intercom.

David W. McFadden lives in Toronto, is the author of several nifty travel books and books of poetry. This is his first blues song.

Don McKay has lived all over Canada. He now lives and writes in B.C., and has had the blues since 1942.

A.F. Moritz is the author of several volumes of poetry, most recently *Rest on the Flight into Egypt* and *Conflicting Desire*. He counts the lyric traditions of folk and popular songs among his influences and has previously written lyrics, some of which have been performed in various modern American popular music genres.

Jane Southwell Munro had heard the blues before Bob, but Bob got her hooked. The music is behind her latest book, *Grief Notes and Animal Dreams*.

P.K. Page is a poet, fiction writer and painter who lives in Victoria. Her latest books are *And Once More Saw the Stars* and *A Kind of Fiction*.

Daria Patriarchus was conceived in Melbourne but born in Alberta. She has published two books of poetry in Australia, *Brand/Name, Generation/X* and *Nietzsche Was Right, Hegel is Dead*, both from X-Press. She works in the import/export business and splits her time between Toronto and Melbourne.

Jay Ruzesky's latest book is *Blue Himalayan Poppies*.

David Seymour's work has appeared in *The Fiddlehead*, *The Malahat Review* and *Ellipse*. He lives in Toronto.

Sue Sinclair grew up in Newfoundland and currently lives in Toronto. Her first book of poems, *Secrets of Weather and Hope*, was published by Brick Books in Spring 2001.

Adam Sol's first book of poetry, *Jonah's Promise*, was published in 2000 by MidList Press. He lives in Toronto with his wife and newborn son.

Karen Solie's first collection of poetry, *Short Haul Engine*, was published by Brick Books this fall. Her fiction appears in *The Journey Prize Anthology 12*, and her creative non-fiction in *Event*.

John Steffler's books of poetry include *That Night We Were Ravenous* (1998), *The Wreckage of Play* (1988) and *The Grey Islands* (1985), reissued by Brick Books in 2001. His novel, *The Afterlife of George Cartwright*, was shortlisted for the Governor General's Award and won the Smithbook/Books in Canada First Novel Award in 1992. He lives in Corner Brook, Newfoundland.

Sharon Thesen most recently is the author of *A Pair of Scissors* and editor of the second edition of *The New Long Poem Anthology*.

Fred Wah has published poetry, prose-poems, biofiction, and criticism and teaches creative writing and poetics at the University of Calgary.

Andy Weaver is doing doctoral work on Canadian and American avant-garde poetry at the University of Alberta. His poetry has appeared in a number of journals, including *Event*, *Grain*, *The Fiddlehead*, and *Prairie Fire*. He is also a founder and coordinating editor of "The Olive", Edmonton's monthly reading series.

Chris Wiseman's most recent book of poetry is *Crossing the Salt Flats* (1999). He lives in Calgary where he started the Creative Writing program at the University of Calgary. Hearing Big Bill Broonzy in a small London club was one of the finest experiences of his life.

Rob Wooldridge lives in Victoria.

Charles Wright's most recent book is *Negative Blue*. He continues to live in Charlottesville, Virginia, and teach at the University of Virginia. He still can't sing a lick.

When not at the extreme ends of the earth, **Rachel Wyatt** lives retiringly in Victoria with her husband Alan and spends her time writing plays and stories and not gardening.

Jan Zwicky has re-strung her gutbucket a couple of times, but they keep telling her not to quit her day job which is in the Philosophy Department at the University of Victoria. Her most recent books are *Songs for Relinquishing the Earth* and *Twenty-One Small Songs*.

NOTES AND ACKNOWLEDGEMENTS

"Speed Blues Junket into Harmonica" by Ken Babstock first appeared in *Days into Flatsptin*, Toronto: House of Anansi Press, 2001.

"thats a lot of suitcases 4 onlee a whil" by bill bissett has been set to music by Bill Roberts, and will appear on the forthcoming CD, *Magik Voices*.

"To Selah" and "King Bee Blues" by George Elliott Clarke first appeared in *Whylah Falls*, Vancouver: Polestar Book Publishers, 1990, 2000.

"Blues for the Blues" by Jannie Edwards appeared in an earlier version in the Edmonton *Stroll of Poets Anthology*, 1999.

"st. mary blues" by Patrick Friesen has been set to music and performed by Big Dave McLean.

"Dashboard Mary" by Ryan Knighton first appeared in *Swing in the Hollow*, Vancouver: Anvil Press, 2001.

"Blues for No-one" by Patrick Lane was originally set to music in 1980 by Sid Marty.

"Riffs" by Dennis Lee first appeared as sections 3, 6, 16, 17, 19, and 20 of *Riffs*, London: Brick Books, 1993.

"Tobacco Belt" by Rick Maddocks was first performed by the author for the Western Theatre Conspiracy cabaret.

The Long Sault was a rapids on the St. Lawrence, which was submerged in the 1950s by a hydroelectric project. "Long Sault Blues" by Don McKay first appeared in *Long Sault*, London: Applegarth Follies, 1975.

"Dada Anna Blue" by Fred Wah was published in an earlier version in Anna Blume and Zaruck (Göttingen: Wallstein Verlag, 2000).

"Dead Pale Penis Person Blues" by Charles Wright first appeared in *Quarter Notes*, Ann Arbor: University of Michigan Press, 1995.

"Laguna Blues" by Charles Wright has appeared in *The Southern Cross*, New York: Random House, 1981 and *The World of the 10,000 Things*, New York: Farrar, Straus, and Giroux, 1990.

"Broke Fiddle Blues" by Jan Zwicky first appeared in *Descant 107*, Volume 30, No. 4 (Winter 1999).

For direct support on this project Smoking Lung Press thanks Linda Cran, Bruce Cran, Barbara Zatyko, Brian Howell, Alma Lee, The Vancouver International Writers Festival, *Geist* Magazine, Jon Wood, Jane Gowan, Teresa McWhirter, Simon Garber, Colin Macleod, Don McKay, Jan Zwicky, Gillian Jerome, and of course Blaine Kyllo, Robert Balantyne and Brian Lam at Arsenal Pulp Press.

MUSIC CREDITS

TRACKS 1—8

Bill Johnson Blues Band

Bill Johnson: all guitars and lead vocals
Casey Dennis: electric and acoustic bass, and background vocals
Gary Preston: piano, and harmonica on tracks 2 and 6
Brendon Hedley: Hammond B3 organ
Jesse Cayhill: drums on tracks 1, 2, 3 and 6
Phil Whipper: drums on tracks 4, 5, 7 and 8

Guest Performers

Dave Harris: violin and harmonica on tracks 3 and 4
Kia Kadiri: rap on track 7
Paul Wainright: alto and tenor saxophone on track 8
Bruce Hurn: trumpet on track 7 and 8

Music written and produced by Bill Johnson
Horn arrangement on "Rainy Lady" by Robert Brodeur
Engineered by Dennis Ferby
Recorded and mixed at Canadian Sound Concepts, Victoria BC, July, 2001
Special thanks to Jan Zwicky and Colin Macleod

TRACKS 9—10

Ken Hamm

Ken Hamm: acoustic guitars, mandolin and vocals

TRACK 11

The Jelly Roll Blues Band

Peter Alan: guitar and vocals
Monte "Harmonica Slim": harmonica

TRACK 12

Six Hands

Rick Maddocks: intercom vocal, guitar, banjo
Jon Wood: lap steel
Geoff Gilliard: percussion

TRACK 13

Jon Wood

Jon Wood: tenor guitar, bass, percussion, xylophone, melodica, organ, dobro, ukulele and electric razor